BHAGAVAD GITA IN 365 DAYS

"The Bhagavad Gita is a true scripture of the human race, a living creation rather than a book, with a new message for every age and a new meaning for every civilization."

–Aurobindo

BHAGAVAD GITA IN 365 DAYS

The Spiritual Essence of the Gita

LATA JAGTIANI

New Age Books

ISBN: 81-7822-256-6

First Edition: Delhi, **2006**

Published by
NEW AGE BOOKS
A-44 Naraina Phase-I
New Delhi-110 028 (INDIA)
Email: nab@vsnl.in
Website: www.newagebooksindia.com

Printed in India
at Shri Jainendra Press
A-45 Naraina Phase-I, New Delhi-110 028

Dedicated to my Satguru
Shri Ramana Maharshi

"The Ordainer controls the fate of souls in accordance with their past deeds, their prarabdha karma. Whatever is destined not to happen will not happen, try how hard you may; whatever is destined to happen will happen, do what you may to stop it. This is certain. The best course, therefore, is for one to be silent."

–Shri Ramana Maharshi

Quotes on the Gita

Albert Einstein–*When I read the Bhagavad Gita and reflect about how God created this universe everything else seems so superfluous.*

Mahatma Gandhi–*The Bhagavad Gita calls on humanity to dedicate body, mind and soul to pure duty and not to become mental voluptuaries at the mercy of random desires and undisciplined impulses.*

When doubts haunt me, when disappointments stare me in the face, and I see not one ray of hope on the horizon, I turn to Gita and find a verse to comfort me; and I immediately begin to smile in the midst of overwhelming sorrow. Those who meditate on the Gita will derive fresh joy and new meanings from it every day.

Aurobindo–*The Bhagavad Gita is a true scripture of the human race, a living creation rather than a book, with a new message for every age and a new meaning for every civilization.*

Henry David Thoreau–*In the morning I bathe my intellect in the stupendous and cosmogonal philosophy of the Bhagavad Gita, in comparison with which our modern world and its literature seems puny and trivial.*

One sentence of the Gita, is worth the State of Massachusetts many times over.

Herman Hesse–*The marvel of the Bhagavad Gita is its truly beautiful revelation of life's wisdom which enables philosophy to blossom into religion.*

Dr. Albert Schweitzer–*The Bhagavad Gita has a profound influence on the spirit of mankind by its devotion to God which is manifested by actions.*

Aldous Huxley–*The Bhagavad Gita is the most systematic statement of spiritual evolution of endowing value to mankind. It is one of the most clear and comprehensive summaries of perennial philosophy ever revealed; hence its enduring value is subject not only to India but to all of humanity.*

Ralph Waldo Emerson–*I owed a magnificent day to the Bhagavad Gita. It was the first of books; it was as if an empire spoke to us, nothing small or unworthy, but large, serene, consistent, the voice of an old intelligence which in another age and climate had pondered and thus disposed of the same questions which exercise us.*

Adi Sankara–*From a clear knowledge of the Bhagavad Gita all the goals of human existence become fulfilled. Bhagavad Gita is the manifest quintessence of all the teachings of the Vedic scriptures.*

A. E. George Russel–*The Bhagavad Gita and the Upanishads contain such godlike fullness of wisdom on all things that I feel the authors must have looked with calm remembrance back through a thousand passionate lives, full of feverish strife for and with shadows, ere they could have written with such certainty of things which the soul feels to be sure.*

Wilhelm von Humboldt–*The Bhagavad Gita is the most beautiful, perhaps the only true philosophical song existing in any known tongue...perhaps the deepest and loftiest thing the world has to show.*

Swami Vivekananda–*You who have read the Gita see all through the book that the one idea is non-attachment. Remain unattached. The other message of the Gita: work, work, work day and night. Flying from work is never the way to find peace. Therefore Krishna teaches us not to shirk our duties but to take them up manfully, and not think of the result.*

Contents

Introduction

To write simply is as difficult as to be good.
—W. Somerset Maugham

As a child when I first heard the Gita's shlokas recited powerfully by Swami Chinmayananda I sensed that the Gita's message was the key to a life of joy and peace. Swamiji, in his characteristic impish style, interspersed the wisdom of the Gita with witty jokes. He succeeded in transforming the formidable Gita into a friend who winked and bantered with me as he gently nudged me away from the darkness of confusion, apathy, fear, and ignorance. Lord Krishna's firm yet caring guidance fell on my ears and I was never the same again. My best friend had arrived. The journey inwards had begun.

Through the years I read various Gita translations, attended several discourses, met spiritual sages and gained insights into the mysterious Gita. Sometimes I was speechless: the answers were all there in black and white and yet we groped around in futility. When I praised the Gita I learnt that many of my friends had not read it because of any of these three reasons. They found the philosophical content too esoteric and were put off by its apparent complexity (in Bombay parlance, it was "high funda"); then some found it too time consuming because of its length (seven hundred verses); finally, they thought it was not presented in simple, understandable English. As a lecturer of English I have heard the same objections against Shakespeare. I appreciated the validity of this objection but wondered what I could do about it. There was nectar in the well of wisdom, there were thirsty people but the bucket they sought was missing. And one day I saw, in my mind's eye, the kind of bucket they were seeking.

When I commuted from my home to the college by train I saw that when the train made an unscheduled stop between stations for a few minutes, while many commuters grumbled about the delay some commuters began to read from a pocket 365-day Bible. I made up my mind to get myself a 365-day Gita. My search drew a blank. There just was no 365-day Gita in all of Mumbai!

The die was cast.

I sensed that my task was an uphill climb and formidable, to say the least. I resolved to think positive and keep my mind focussed on a step at a time up the steep mountain. I was guided to do my dharma by the Gita's

Chapter 3 verse:

"It is infinitely better to do one's own duty, however deficiently one does it, than to do another's duty however perfectly one performs it. Even if it were to require one's giving up one's very life for it, it is better to do one's own duty. To do another's duty is dangerous."

It took me nine years of research and plodding forward a step at a time to create a friendly, simple, easy to understand English Gita in easy-to-carry size. A Gita easy to carry, easy to comprehend, easy to gift, easy to afford and easy to put in the briefcase or on the bedside. Anybody over twelve years of age curious about the meaning and direction of life, both Hindu and non-Hindu alike, can read it and enhance his life with its wisdom.

"Bhagavad Gita in 365 Days: The Spiritual Essence of the Gita" is an attempt to fill the void that has existed for far too long. I would be delighted to get both critical as well as appreciative responses from you.

I am deeply grateful to my husband, Manek Premchand, for his patient suggestions, to Shisham Hinduja for her creative inputs for the book-cover, to Arthur Thorley for replacing my Indianisms with "propah" English.

LATA JAGTIANI
Email: latashea@yahoo.com

Background

The Gita consists of 700 verses and is the philosophical component of the great Indian epic, "The Mahabharata". It is essentially about the great war that was fought by the Bharata race, north of Delhi, India, approximately between 1200 B.C. and 3021 B.C.

The three Bharata children, Dhritarashtra, Pandu and Vidura were brought up by their uncle Bhishma who was the acting king. When they came of age, one of them had to ascend the throne. Since the eldest, Dhritarashtra was blind, the throne went to Pandu who had five sons, Yudhishthira, Bhima, Arjuna, Nakul and Sahadeva. When Pandu died they were still young and their kind uncle Dhritarashtra took charge of them. Dhritarashtra himself had a hundred sons who were called the Kauravas while the five brothers were known as the Pandavas. All the Pandava children were educated with kindness by Dhritarashtra along with his own sons, the hundred Kauravas.

Sadly, with time disputes and dislikes arose between the Kauravas and the Pandavas and the animosity and hatred multiplied. The Kauravas, headed by the eldest

Duryodhana, were proud and insolent to the five cousins. When Dhritarashtra nominated the eldest Pandava, Yudhishthira, as the heir apparent it enraged the Kauravas. Duryodhana wanted to destroy his cousins and plotted to set fire to their home; however they received a timely warning from their well-meaning uncle Vidura and they escaped. The Kauravas believed their enemies had perished in the fire but the Pandavas fled and lived in disguise in the forest. Later, they were discovered and Dhritarashtra recalled his nephews to court and divided his kingdom between his sons and his nephews.

The Pandavas worked hard and their kingdom prospered but the Kauravas wanted to contain their power. They were invited to a game of dice where the Kauravas, through cheating, robbed the Pandavas of everything, almost including their common wife, Draupadi, who was saved in the nick of time by Lord Krishna's intervention.

The Pandavas played one last game which required them to go into exile for 13 years if they lost. They lost. They left and in the 13th year of exile they worked with King Virata and helped him repel attacks on his kingdom by the Kauravas. Once the exile period expired they returned to claim their kingdom which the Kauravas refused. The battle-lines were drawn with the

Pandavas being determined and soon various kings supported either the Kauravas or the Pandavas. The blind king Dhritarashtra was unhappy but helpless. King Krishna was related to both the cousins and wanted to take no sides. However the Kauravas gladly chose his offer of his army to work with them while the Pandavas happily accepted his offer of accompanying them on the chariot through the war.

Since the King was blind, the Lord granted special vision to Sanjaya to recount whatever transpired on the battlefield and the Gita is a narration to the King by Sanjaya. The Gita commences with Arjuna wavering when he sees his cousins on the opposite side, saying to Lord Krishna that he does not feel like shedding the blood of his own kith and kin.

The Gita is a conversation between the bewildered and despondent Arjuna and the clear-headed and sagacious Krishna who explains to Arjuna why the battle must be fought by him, even if his own cousins perish as a consequence. The meaning of duty, life, death, honor, truth, wisdom, etc., are explained by Lord Krishna to the confused Arjuna. The eighteenth chapter is the concluding chapter in which Arjuna gains clarity and declares his readiness for battle. The Gita ends here and the battle of the Mahabharata commences.

Who's who in the Bhagavad Gita

Lord Krishna: The incarnation of Lord Vishnu who takes birth to destroy evil and establish righteousness. He was born to Vasudeva, the brother of queen Kunti. As a cousin to both the Pandavas and the Kauravas he gave the Pandavas his own presence as a charioteer and the Kauravas his fully equipped army. As the charioteer the Lord instructs the confused and faint-hearted Arjuna to pick up his bow and commence fighting.

Arjuna: The third of the Pandava brothers, the most valiant of them. He was the son of Kunti and the Lord Indra. He studied archery under Dronacharya and became his best pupil of the Pandavas and the Kauravas.

Yudhishthira: Eldest of the five Pandavas, was the embodiment of truth, justice, compassion and righteousness. His only weakness was the game of dice which led to the exile of the Pandavas and the subsequent Mahabharata war.

Bhima: Second of the Pandava brothers, renowned for his super-human strength and voracious appetite, fearlessness and might.

Duryodhana: The head of the Kauravas, eldest son of blind king Dhritarashtra and Gandhari, evil in intent and coarse in conduct. He was the main adversary of the Pandavas.

Dhritarashtra: Father of the Kauravas, uncle to the Pandavas. He was blind but a just and kind man.

Bhishma: Son of Ganga and Devavrata, was graced with the boon that he would live as long as he wished and death would come to him only when he desired it. This grandsire and respected head of both the Pandava and Kaurava families led the Kauravas in battle. His might was awesome and yet he constantly asked Duryodhana to make peace with the Pandavas but failed.

Dronacharya: Teacher of warring skills such as archery to both the Pandavas and the Kauravas. Very respected and loved by both, his favourite pupil was Arjuna of the Pandavas although in battle he was with the Kauravas.

Sanjaya: Devoted and trusted counsellor of Dhritarashtra, Vyasa granted him the power to see and hear everything that was taking place on the battle-field as if he were physically present at Kurukshetra. He gave a truthful account of the battle to blind king Dhritarashtra.

Chapter One

Jan 1

On the field of Kurukshetra, a battle
Was about to commence between two forces:
Between those who upheld righteous conduct
And those that did not.

Sanjaya had been graced by the Infinite Spirit
With super-human vision
To see from afar all the events
That transpired on the battlefield
And to recount them
To blind king Dhritarashtra
So he might be well informed.

Jan 2

The war on the battlefield of Kurukshetra
Was between the Kauravas
Headed by Duryodhana, son of Dhritarashtra,
And the Pandavas headed by Arjuna,
Whose charioteer was Lord Krishna.

Jan 3

Sanjaya started to recount:
Seeing the Pandava army well arrayed,
Duryodhana tells Dronacharya,
His martial arts teacher:

"Behold how mighty appear the Pandavas,
Although we know them to be no match for us
Even then, somehow, they appear very strong;
On the other hand, by comparison,
Although our side is really stronger
Both in range and depth,
It, nevertheless, seems weaker.

Jan 4

"The army of the Pandavas,
Although marshalled only by Bhima,
Appears formidable;
While our army despite being mightily headed
By the incomparable Bhishma,
Appears inadequate and incapable of victory.

Jan 5

"Therefore, let all the soldiers
Form a circular ring around Bhishma,
Who is the Kaurava heart;
Bhishma must be protected,
He is at the very core of our strength."

After hearing this, the mighty Bhishma
Blew on the conch as loud as a lion's roar,
Announcing to the Pandavas
The readiness of the Kauravas
For battle.

Jan 6

On the other side, across the battlefield,
The Pandavas and the charioteer Krishna,
Immediately responded by blowing
Their own conches
Signalling to the Kauravas
Their own readiness for battle;
Their powerful and loud response
Made the Kauravas feel fearful.
The Pandava response filled
The earth below and the sky around
With powerful, surging sound.

Jan 7

Seeing the readiness of both sides
For the fight,
The brave Pandava warrior, Arjuna,
Was immediately plagued by doubts
He wondered if it was right
That cousins should fight
And kill one another
Merely for family honor?

Jan 8

Then the despondent Arjuna said to Krishna:
"When I see my family,
Arrayed gladly on the opposite side,
All ready to fight,
My limbs weaken, my mouth goes dry,
My body trembles, my hair stands on end,
My skin burns, and the bow slips from my arms.
I cannot be steady, my mind reels.

Jan 9

"O Krishna, I long
Neither for victory nor for kingdom
Nor even for earthly pleasures.
Of what use, to the Pandavas,
Is kingdom, or enjoyment,
Or even life, at such a high cost?

Jan 10

"These, my kinsmen,
I wouldn't consent to kill,
Even were they to come to kill me,
I wouldn't do so even if, in exchange,
I was to be offered the boon
Of the kingdom of the three worlds,
Of earth, heaven and atmosphere.

Why, then, should I go forward
And try to destroy,
My own cousins and peers
Only for earthly reasons?

Jan 11

"Why should we not, instead,
Have the wisdom to refuse to sin,
We, who can plainly see the wrong,
In the annihilation of our own?

Jan 12

"It would be far better,
At least for me,
If were they to attack me,
I should collapse and be killed,
Succumbing to death,
Unresisting and unarmed."

Having spoken thus, Arjuna sank down
On the chariot, and despondently cast aside
His soldier's bow and arrow,
His spirit overwhelmed by sorrow.

Chapter Two

Jan 13

Sanjaya said to Dhritarashtra:

To him thus overcome with pity,
Whose eyes were tearful,
Who seemed troubled,
And very despondent,
Lord Krishna, the charioteer, spoke thus:

"From where has this dejection
Of spirits come to you, O Arjuna,
In this hour of crisis ?
It neither suits men of noble natures
Nor does it lead to heaven;
In fact, it causes nothing but disgrace;
So cast off this faint-heartedness
And arise!"

Jan 14

Arjuna asked Lord Krishna:

"How, O my Lord Krishna,
Shall I assault Dronacharya and Bhishma,
Strike down those that I like?
They deserve my respect and yet you advise me
To put them away;
How can I kill those same people
Who taught me these very warring skills?
Should I use the knowledge
That they imparted to me
Now to destroy them?

Jan 15

"In this world it is better to live
Even as homeless beggars,
Than to kill one's honored teachers.
I cannot act.
I am, in fact,
Immobilized and paralyzed.

After having killed these teachers,
Can I ever hope for any joy
That will be untainted by
The memory of their bloody deaths?
I cannot carry out these killings
Of my teachers and siblings.

Jan 16

"With my mind bewildered about my duty,
I ask you, O Krishna, guide me,
I am your pupil, I beseech you,
Teach me, show me,
I who seek refuge and solace,
Finally only in you."

Sanjaya said:

Having thus addressed Krishna,
The mighty Arjuna, in despair, added:
"I will not fight"
And became silent.

Jan 17

Lord Krishna now addressed
Arjuna who was so depressed,
Calmly guiding and soothing,
His friend who was hurting:

"You grieve for those
For whom you should not grieve,
And yet I understand your doubts.
Wise men grieve neither for the dead
Nor for those that are living.

Jan 18

"O Arjuna, remember always,
Never was there a time
When I was not, or you were not,
Or these Kauravas were not.
Nor will there ever come a time,
When any of us shall cease to be.

Jan 19

"As the soul passes in this body
Through childhood, youth and age,
Even while this continues,
It is also readying itself
To take on another form;
The wise ones know
How these things go.

Jan 20

"You are troubled and you worry
About matters temporary.
Heat, cold, pain, pleasure
Are only physical reactions to sensations:
They begin, and they end.
They exist merely momentarily.
Learn to recognize and be wise
That it is they alone that prevent
Your spiritual evolution
And block you from attaining
Your final freedom.

Jan 21

"The one who is untroubled by
Pain and pleasure,
Such a one alone is fit for immortality.

Jan 22

"That which is not
Shall never be;
That which is
Shall never cease to be.
To the truth-seer these truths
Are self-evident.

Jan 23

"There is a common element
That dwells in all that you see;
It is the all-pervading Infinite Spirit.
O Arjuna, always know,
That nothing can ever destroy
The imperishable Spirit.

Jan 24

"Both persons,
The one who believes
That the Spirit destroys,
And the one who thinks
That it can be destroyed,
Both of them are ignorant.

Jan 25

"The Spirit neither kills,
Nor ever gets killed.
The Spirit was never born,
It will never die;
Nor once having been,
Can it ever cease to be.

Jan 26

"This Spirit is unborn and eternal,
Permanent and changeless,
It does not die
Even when the flesh dies.

Jan 27

"How can the one who understands
The indestructible nature of this Spirit,
How can that one ever accept
That the Spirit can be killed,
When it is, by its very nature,
Imperishable, indestructible?

Jan 28

"Like one who discards worn-out garments,
Replacing them with new ones,
In the same manner,
The embodied soul
Casts off the old worn-out body
And dons a fresh, new form.

Jan 29

"This Spirit is imperishable,
Weapons cannot wound it,
Fire cannot burn it,
Water cannot wet it,
And wind cannot dry it.
It is indestructible.

Jan 30

"This indestructible Spirit
Cannot be drowned, scorched or dried.
It is eternal and unchanging.

Jan 31

"And even if you think that
One is perpetually born
And perpetually dies,
Even then, O Arjuna,
You should not grieve.

Feb 1

"Most certain
Is the death of the born,
And also most certain
Is the birth of the dead;
Therefore, grieve not
For something that is inevitable.
For this Spirit, in every body,
Is imperishable.

Feb 2

"Thus you ought not to grieve
For the physical death of any mortal;
For physical death is inevitable
For all earthly creations.

Feb 3

But remember at all times-
You must never falter
In doing your duty.
You must never shirk it
At any cost.

Feb 4

"You know that for a soldier
There is no higher duty
Than to fight a just war;
But if you, as a soldier,
Refuse to do your duty
You will do wrong
And then down the years
People will narrate your tale
With deep shame and pain.

Feb 5

"For you who has been so much honored,
It is far worse than death
That later generations take your name
With sorrow and shame,
Recounting your act of running from battle
As a dishonored fact, a bad memory;
And that they use you as an example
Of a dishonorable man.

Feb 6

"All of them will recall
With both anger and gall,
Your refusal to fight
As the coward's flight
Not motivated by ethics but by fear.
By refusing to do your duty
You are incurring the wrath
Of many a noble, righteous heart.

Feb 7

"But if, during the brave fight,
While doing right,
You lose your life,
You attain to a higher bliss;
And if, because of your bravery,
You taste laudable victory,
All honors will be due,
And in history your name
Will be amongst the very few.

Therefore, arise, O Arjuna,
And fight!

Feb 8

"With equal unconcern
You must regard both sensations
Of pleasure and pain,
Loss and gain,
Victory and defeat.
In that spirit
Ready yourself for battle;
Thus alone will you not
Commit any wrong.

Feb 9

"To break out from this cycle of action,
It is important for you to understand
Both paths-
The path of knowledge
And the path of action.
Effort is neither wasted
Nor can it be counter-productive
On the path of true action.
Even a little of its practice
Protects one from great danger.

Feb 10

"Remember, O Arjuna,
You have a right only to action
And never to the fruits of action.

Feb 11

"Let not the fruits of action
Ever be your motive,
But also never let there be
Any attachment to inaction.

Feb 12

"Do your work, O Arjuna,
Fixed in righteous action.
Always be guarded against attachment,
You must evenly regard both
Success and failure.
The essence of yoga
Is even-mindedness.

Feb 13

"O Arjuna, mere action is inferior
To unattached action,
Seek therefore refuge
In detached yet dutiful action.

Feb 14

"I pity those that act
For gain, return or reward.

Feb 15

"When your intelligence
Has guided you to non-attachment
And made you unperturbed
By what you've heard
Or what you haven't,
You will have then overcome
The wall of delusion."

Feb 16

Arjuna asked:
"Such a wise person
As you would wish me to be,
My lord, how can one recognise
This man who is wise,
Whose being is non-attached?
How does such a one talk, sit, walk?"

Feb 17

The Lord answered:
"When one puts away
The passions of the mind,
And when one is entirely content
With one's real spirit,
One can be regarded as a person
Possessing secure understanding.

Feb 18

"The one whose mind
Is untroubled by sorrows
And longs not for joys,
And the one who is free
From all passion, fear or wrath,
Such a one can be called
The sage of secure understanding.

Feb 19

"Wherever such a wise one goes
There is attachment to none.
This one accepts alike
Both good and evil
With equanimity;
The understanding of such a one
Is secure.

Feb 20

"Such a one consciously
Pulls back the senses
From desirable objects,
Like the tortoise, seeing danger approach,
Withdraws into its shell-
He has secure understanding.
Holding all the senses in check,
He will sit intent on me.
For, with senses under control,
Secure understanding is possible.

Feb 21

"When one dwells on sense-objects,
Attachment for them arises,
From attachment springs desire,
And from desire comes anger,
From anger arises confusion,
And from that arises loss of memory.
All these cause
The destruction of intelligence,
And such sad, deep distress
Makes one's state hopeless,
And takes one even further away
From spiritual freedom.

Feb 22

"But a person of disciplined mind,
Although he moves among sense objects
He always does so with his senses under control,
He thus remains free from
Both attachment and aversion.
Such a one can attain purity of spirit.

Feb 23

"In the purity of spirit
Is the end of all sorrow;
The person with senses in rein,
Will surely gain
Peace of mind.

Feb 24

"Every day the ocean receives
Waters of all rivers
And yet does not overflow,
Keeping itself in check
And containing itself on both sides;
Similarly, the peaceful one,
Towards whom desires are directed
Remains steadfast and unperturbed
And exercises wise restraint
And does not get carried away.

Feb 25

"When the mind begins
To follow the wandering senses,
Understanding gets swept away,
Just as easily as the wind
Which carries adrift
A ship on the ocean's waters.

Feb 26

"Therefore, O Arjuna,
The one whose senses
Are withdrawn from sense-objects-
That one alone
Has secure understanding.

Feb 27

"When it is night-time
For all other mortals,
It is the right time
For the extraordinary one
To open his eyes and awaken;
On the other hand,
When all others are awake
It is night for the wise sage.

Feb 28

"He who abandons all desires
And whose actions are free from longing,
Without any sense of 'I' and 'mine',
He has attained peace of mind.
Once a person attains this state,
The peace that comes with it
Can never be taken from him
Even at the time of his death.
He will remain firmly centered
And will become one with the eternal."

Chapter Three

Mar 1

Arjuna asked:
"If wisdom is superior to action,
Then why are you urging me
To actions that kill?
This contradiction bewilders me."

Mar 2

Krishna replied:
"O Arjuna, in this world
There is a two-fold path:
There is the path of wisdom
For those that meditate,
And the path of selfless action
For those that perform;
But neither of them gets
Freedom from action
By refraining from action.

Mar 3

"Nor can they attain perfection
By refraining from action;
For it is impossible for anyone
To live a life without action.
All are helplessly driven to action
By the force of nature.

Mar 4

"The one who restrains
The organs of actions,
But yet remains in mind
Brooding over the temptations
Is but a hypocrite
Who deludes none but himself.

Mar 5

"On the other hand,
The one who controls the senses
By harnessing the mind,
Is honest and truthful.

Mar 6

"Therefore you must always do your duty
Through righteous action.
Action undertaken for the sake of duty,
Is superior to inaction;
And by being inactive,
O Arjuna, you know only too well,
That it is impossible to dwell
Even in the physical realm.

Mar 7

"Futile is the life
Of the one who is unaware
Of the wheel and its revolution,
Who lives merely to wallow
In senses that are shallow.

Mar 8

"The gods have created
Various parts and elements of life
For all to gain,
One from the other,
Each to benefit another;
But the one who takes from nature
Without giving to it in return
Can be defined a thief.

Mar 9

"All creatures great and small
Are nurtured by food,
And food is born of rain;
Rain comes out of the sacrifice
Which is born of work.
The one not contributing
To this blessed cycle lives in vain,
He lives merely to indulge his senses.

Mar 10

"But for the individual
Who is one with the Supreme Spirit,
And who is content with this union,
For such a one deeds are not fetters;
Such a one has no interest whatever
To gain by actions
And no interest, moreover,
In unperformed actions.
Therefore, without attachment,
Always perform your righteous duty.

Mar 11

"The good king Janaka, Sita's father,
Like others, attained to perfection thus.
All the work that one does
Must be done with the thought
Of maintaining the world
And keeping in motion
This necessary cycle.

Mar 12

"For it is written that individuals attain
To the highest possible gain
When doing their duty with no personal motive
And with no real attachment.
People imitate superior beings
Following their examples;
So, as an example,
If I, too, stopped working,
Men will cease functioning,
And if I stopped working,
The three worlds would crumble,
Judgement would blur, chaos would follow
And all beings would perish.

Mar 13

"All actions are performed
By the qualities of nature;
The one who thinks with conceit
That it is he that is the wilful doer
And he does it alone,
Is nothing but an egoist loser.

Mar 14

"Thus, surrendering to me,
Your thoughts concentrating on me,
And without any anticipation of reward,
With a mind empty of excitement,
Act in righteous earnest,
And begin, O Arjuna,
Begin your fight!

Mar 15

"Even the knowledgeable ones
Act according to their essential nature.
All creatures follow their nature,
What is the use, then, of pointless doubt
About performing what is one's righteous duty?

Mar 16

"All senses have their likes and dislikes
But one must not be swayed by them
Since they only succeed
In obstructing one from
The realisation of Truth.

Mar 17

"It is infinitely better
To do one's own duty
However deficiently one does it,
Than to do another's duty
However perfectly one performs it;
Even if it were to require one's giving up
One's very life for it.
It is better to do one's own duty.
To do another's duty is dangerous."

Mar 18

Arjuna asked:
"Then what forces a man
To sin against his own will?"

Mar 19

The Lord answered:
"The individual sins
Because of desire,
Because of wrath,
Born of passion.
They consume and corrupt everything,
They are our enemies.

Mar 20

"Desire is the wise one's constant enemy,
It mars the face of wisdom.
It is as insatiable as a flame.
Therefore, O Arjuna,
Control your senses from the start
And steer away from this strong force.
This is the starting-point of all the troubles
In one's life.

Chapter Four

Mar 21

"I have had many lives
And so have you, O Arjuna,
But while I know of all of them
You know them not.
While I am unborn and imperishable
I am yet born through my own will
Into this material world.

Mar 22

"Whenever right declines,
Whenever wrong flourishes,
Then, O Arjuna,
I reincarnate myself,
To protect the good
And to destroy the bad.

Mar 23

"I come down in human form
To re-establish righteousness;
I thus come into being
From age to age.

Mar 24

"The one who realises this truth
Concerning my life and death,
The one who learns about the life
That never ends in death,
That one is never born again.
Upon leaving the body
That one merges with me.

Mar 25

"Freed from passion,
Fear and anger,
Filled with me,
Relying only on me,
Purified in the fire of wisdom,
Many have entered into my being.

Mar 26

"I satisfy all seekers,
Irrespective of the path
Chosen by them to reach me;
O Arjuna, all the righteous paths
However different they may seem,
Are all mine.

Mar 27

"Actions do not affect me,
Nor do I desire the fruit of action;
The one who understands this
Is not bound by actions.

Mar 28

"It is essential to understand
What is right action.
What is wrong action,
What is inaction,
For, to you,
All this is, indeed, mysterious.

Mar 29

"The one who sees
Inaction in action
And action in inaction
Is the wisest of all:
Such a one is a sage.

Mar 30

"The wise call
This one a sage,
Since everything done by him
Is free from any attachment
To the fruits of action.
Always content, independent,
Such a one, though immersed in action,
Yet acts not;
Expecting nothing,
He is, thus, untainted.

Mar 31

"Such a wise one is satisfied
With whatever occurs even by accident,
And remains unbound and free
From petty envy and small jealousy;
He is ever free from the extremes
Of pleasure and pain.

Apr 1

"He, the wise one, is free from attachment,
His mind is free from ignorance,
He does righteous deeds as an offering
To the Divine Spirit,
All his work is nothing but a sacrifice
To the Divine Spirit.

Apr 2

"People offer different things as sacrifice,
Some offer material things,
Others make severe vows,
Some offer knowledge and scholarship,
Some control their breath,
While others control their food;
These persons try to make amends
For their errors and sins.

Apr 3

"Knowledge of the final truth
Offered as a sacrifice
Is greater than all material sacrifices;
Obtain wisdom, therefore,
So that you may be released
From the cycle of re-birth.
Once you know this
You will be free from doubt,
And regard everything alive around,
As part of yourself and thus,
As an inevitable part of me.

Apr 4

"The wise man accepts all that happens
And his mind is unaffected
By both pain and pleasure;
He remains unbound
By both positive and negative consequences.
He remains unaffected,
He rises after the performance
Of the righteous act,
Having done his own righteous duty.

Apr 5

"Even if one is the most unrighteous,
And even if one has neglected one's duty,
And even if one is the greatest wrong-doer,
One may yet cross over to the other side
From evil to good
If one travels aboard
The ferryboat of wisdom.

Apr 6

"Just as the lit fire turns its fuel to ashes,
In the same manner
The fire of wisdom and true knowledge,
Turns to ashes all the embers of action and work,
However unrighteous the doer's past work was.

Apr 7

"There is nothing in the world
As purifying as wisdom.
And the one who has attained it
Shall quickly attain supreme peace;
But the one who doubts,
Lacking both knowledge and faith,
That one truly loses.

Apr 8

"For the being that is ignorant
There is neither this world,
Nor the one beyond,
Nor happiness.

Apr 9

"Thus, O beloved Arjuna,
With the decisive sword of wisdom,
Sever this doubt,
Bred of ignorance,
That has crept into your heart.
Follow the path of wisdom
O great warrior,
And arise!"

Chapter Five

Apr 10

Arjuna asked:
"At one moment you praise
Renunciation of work,
And at another you laud
Performance of righteous action;
Tell me which one of these
Is better for one's welfare."

Apr 11

Lord Krishna replied:
"Both attain to the supreme state;
But of the two
The detached performance
Of right action is better.

Apr 12

"The one who never dislikes
And the one who never desires–
Who is not affected by these opposites–
That one can be called a true ascetic,
His is true renunciation.

Apr 13

"To the ignorant,
The renunciation of action
And its performance are separate,
But not to the wise;
The one who understands well
Even one of the two
Gets the fruit of both;
Both of them bear the same result.

Apr 14

"Only the ignorant speak of the two
As distinct and separate;
Both wisdom and right action
Lead to the same conclusion.

Apr 15

"Without concentration, O Arjuna,
Renunciation is difficult;
But the one who meditates steadily,
Will realize the nature of the eternal reality.

Apr 16

"An individual who understands
That the highest self is common to all,
That individual, even in action,
Is not bound by action
And its results.

Apr 17

"Though this wise one sees, hears, touches,
Smells, eats, moves, sleeps and breathes,
The awareness of the truth remains
As a constant refrain,
Ever reminding, ever alerting,
That the doer is the higher self,
And not the ego-bound lower self.

Apr 18

"Though this sage talks,
Gives and receives,
Opens and shuts the eyes,
The awareness remains
That these are but the senses
Reacting to perceptions.

Apr 19

"The wise perform all acts dispassionately
And without any personal attachment,
And thus win eternal peace,
Just as a lotus-leaf is untouched
By the dirty water around it.

Apr 20

"But the one who acts for reward,
Is firmly held and imprisoned.

Apr 21

"The dispassionate one neither acts
Nor causes others to act.
The Supreme Spirit is not responsible
For either the virtue
Or the sin
Of any egoistic doer.

Apr 22

"The one who knows the Absolute
And remains resolute,
Who feels no loss or gain,
Neither joy nor pain,
He can unite with the Supreme.
People are often deluded
When they see ignorance
Covered as wisdom;
But like the sun,
The Supreme Spirit will shine through
And make itself visible
To those whose wisdom
Has destroyed ignorance.

Apr 23

"Devoted fully to their higher self,
Meditating on it,
Losing themselves in it,
Having dissolved their sins
With the power of their wisdom-
Such individuals reach the place
From where there is no return.

Apr 24

"Having understood the scriptures correctly
The wise one sees equally
A person of learning and humility
And regards with the same respect
A cow, a dog or an elephant,
Putting all, including the outcaste,
On the same level
Being always mindful of the fact
That all beings are inhabited
By the same Supreme Spirit.

Apr 25

"The wise one neither rejoices at pleasant events,
Nor grieves at unpleasant ones.
His equanimity is steady at all times.

Apr 26

"While relating to outside forces,
Happiness and sadness occur;
All these begin and all these end;
The wise one keeps away from both feelings.

Apr 27

"The one who is firm in understanding
And is established in the Supreme;
Finding happiness within the Self
Enjoying eternal peace,
This one has no desire for earthly contact.

Apr 28

"The pleasures of earthly contact
Are only sources of sorrow,
And realising that all pleasures and sorrows
Must always begin and end,
The wise one stays unmoved by them.

Apr 29

"Unattached to external objects
The wise one finds joy within,
And earns unity with the Almighty.

Apr 30

"Before leaving the physical body
If one is able to surmount these desires
One can be assured of supreme joy.

May 1

"One should be content with oneself
And allow the inner light to shine
Influencing all that is done,
Leaving no space vacant
For sorrows to occupy.

May 2

"Subdue the base instincts
Recognise that you are not distinct
From other creatures.
This will give peace
To your troubled mind.

May 3

"By controlling all senses
And by harnessing the wandering mind,
The persistent sage may soon find
Freedom from the binding mind.
Soon the sage can receive
The joy of eternal peace."

Chapter Six

May 4

Lord Krishna continued:
"The one who acts
Without motivation of reward
Has truly renounced.

May 5

"There are those that refuse
To light the sacred fire
And there are those that refuse
To perform sacred rituals;
But by merely denying these acts
One cannot be called a renunciate,
Since by refusing to perform deeds outwardly
One does not become a renunciate.

May 6

"Unless selfish action
Has been renounced,
None can become spiritual.
One must give up
Doing deeds for rewards
And one must perform
Detached yet disciplined activity.

May 7

"One must be unattached to both,
The objects of sense,
And to the fruits of one's acts.
One must renounce
All expectation of reward
Resulting from one's deeds.
Such a one alone
Can be said to have attained
True spirituality.

May 8

"Aided by the higher Self,
The wise one must always strive to improve,
And to be true to the same Self.
The one who heeds that higher Self
Will never be alone
Since it is a constant friend,
A friend who is always near at hand.

May 9

"But if the individual
Does not heed the Supreme Self,
He will soon know
He has a constant foe.

May 10

"The one who is impartial
To both friend and foe,
And sits neutrally among
Both aliens and relatives,
Whether they be sinners or saints,
That one has attained excellence.

May 11

"When one has mastered
One's lower self,
And when one can be content alone
With one's real Self,
Then one finds peace
Whether there be
Heat or cold,
Pleasure or pain,
Respect or disrespect.

May 12

"The seeker of spirituality
Must unceasingly strive
To concentrate on the Spirit
In seclusion, all alone,
With complete control
Over mind and body both,
Freed from hope and greed,
Equally regarding both–
Ordinary stones and gold.

May 13

"To overcome this baser self
The seeker must practice meditation
With peace in the heart
And fearlessness in the mind
Concentrating only on me.
Thus shall peace be attained.
This, in turn, will lead one
To ultimate freedom.

May 14

"Meditation is not meant
For those among men
Who eat too much,
Or don't eat at all,
Or for those that
Sleep too much
Or don't sleep at all.

May 15

Meditation is only for those
Who can and do regulate food,
Regulate recreation,
Regulate sleep;
It is meant for those
Whose actions are restrained,
And who are disciplined in deeds.

May 16

"The wise one who has conquered the mind
And is ever absorbed in the Supreme Self
Is like a small *diya* (lamp)
Which cannot flicker
In a windless atmosphere,
But burns on steadily and serenely.
The passions of the mind,
The desires, are like the wind
Which disturb and prevent the *diya*
From doing it's duty
Of brightening everything around it.

May 17

"The wise one calmly rests
Within the Supreme Self
And always stays on the righteous way.
He carefully guards this Self
As his most precious possession
Since by possessing it no calamity occurs;
Once he does this no event has any impact at all.

May 18

"When the wavering mind
Begins to wander
The wise one can restrain it
And bring it back successfully
Into the domain of the Supreme Self.

May 19

"For supreme bliss can be enjoyed
Only by such a wise one
Whose mind is tranquil,
Whose passions are controlled,
Who is sinless,
And who has become one
With the Eternal.

May 20

"Only then can a wise one
See the same Spirit in all beings,
And all beings in the same Spirit;
This wise one sees everywhere
Nothing but the Supreme Spirit.

May 21

"The wise one sees me in everything
And everything in me;
Him I can never forsake
Nor can he ever lose me."

May 22

Arjuna asked:
"I don't see how I can attain
This state of serene poise,
When I am so restless in mind,
And cannot find a permanent solution
To my turbulent situation.
O Krishna, it is just as difficult
As trying to restrain the blowing wind."

May 23

Krishna replied:
"Yes, the mind is difficult to control,
But, with repeated practice,
And repeated renunciation,
It can always be possible
If one only adopts the right ways."

May 24

Arjuna asked:
"But what happens to the one
Who fails to control,
What of him, O Krishna?"

May 25

Krishna replied:
"My beloved child,
Even then no evil awaits you,
If you have scrupulously
Followed the path of righteous duty.

May 26

"Having been, for many years,
On the righteous path,
The one who slips from spirituality
Will yet be born again,
In a family that is pure,
Or very rarely, in a family of wisdom;
Then his past experiences become
The starting point towards the goal of perfection;
Thus nothing is lost, but is accumulated
Towards the next birth.

May 27

"Then after many lives,
The seeker of spirituality
Whose sins are absolved
Attains perfection
And finally reaches
The Supreme Being.

May 28

"The wise one is superior to all,
The ascetic, the scholar,
And the man of action.
Therefore, O Arjuna,
Be a wise one!

Chapter Seven

May 29

"Among the thousands of people
Scarcely one strives for perfection
And of those that strive and succeed,
Scarcely one knows me in truth.

May 30

"My nature is made of eight elements
Earth, water, fire, air, sky,
Mind, intellect and ego;
This is my lower nature,
But know that my higher nature
Is distinct from this, O Arjuna!

May 31

"I am the origin of the world
And I will be its dissolution;
There is nothing higher than me.
All that exists is strung around me
As rows of gems on a string.

Jun 1

"I am the salt-taste of the ocean,
I am the light in the sun and moon.

Jun 2

"I am the syllable 'OM' in the Vedas,
I am the sound in ether,
I am the manliness of man,
I am the fragrance of the earth.

Jun 3

"I am the brightness of the fire,
I am the life force in all that exists,
I am the austerity in the ascetics,
I am the undying seed of all beings.

Jun 4

"I am the intelligence of the intelligent,
I am the splendor of the splendid.
I am the strength of the strong
Who are free from both attachment and desire.

Jun 5

"I am the urge towards righteousness.
Whether they be pure, passionate or ignorant,
The urges are all derived from me.
They are in me,
But I am not in all of them.

Jun 6

"The sinner, the ignorant, the evil,
The one deprived of spiritual insight,
Being blinded by glamorous illusion,
And the ones who choose the evil life-
None of these, O Arjuna,
Shall reach and find me.

Jun 7

"O Arjuna, there are four kinds
Of good people that worship me:
The suffering ones,
The ones thirsting for knowledge,
The ones desirous of learning truth
And finally those that desire wisdom;
Although all are noble-minded,
The highest is the wise one,
Who meditates on me without ceasing.
For I am very beloved to him
And he is very beloved to me.

Jun 8

"The wise one who recognizes
The Supreme Spirit
Everywhere and in everything,
Indeed, is rare to find.

Jun 9

"If the seeker uses even one path
With sincere faith,
Then shall his desires find
Fulfilment through that same path
For thus have I ordained.

Jun 10

"The one who is limited in insight
Correspondingly obtains limited fruit.
The ignorant think that I am just human form
When, in fact, I am the unmanifest;
They do not realize
My nature is changeless and spiritual.

Jun 11

"The inhabitants of this earth
Deluded by illusion
Neither realise nor correctly recognise
My true nature –
That I am higher than the highest
And that I am changeless.

Jun 12

"I know all beings
Past, present and future,
But they do not know me.
Only the wise know me.

Jun 13

"Their acts, being righteous,
Their sins having been destroyed,
Their worship of me firmly resolved,
These wise ones live in me
Even in the crucial hour
Of their earthly death."

Chapter Eight

Jun 14

Arjuna asked:
"Tell me about the Supreme Spirit,
The nature of the Self,
And the nature of action.
What is the domain of matter
And what is divinity?"

Jun 15

Krishna answered:
"The Supreme Spirit, the absolute,
Is the indestructible Self;
The worlds have been created
And are supported by this creative force alone
Which brings all beings into this world.

Jun 16

"All matter is form that perishes
While divinity is that which does not;
That individual always enters my being
Who, at the time of his physical death,
When casting off the body,
Thinks of me.

Jun 17

"But whoever, in the end,
Thinks of any mortal being
To that being alone
That one shall go.

Jun 18

"Thus, at all times,
If you wish to unite with me,
Think of me.
All the gates of the body
Should be restrained and controlled,
The mind should be locked in the
Innermost heart,
The breath fixed within the head,
Rapt in meditation.

Jun 19

"The one who utters
The single syllable 'OM'
Which stands for Brahman,
Remembering me as the body dies,
Attains to the highest bliss.

Jun 20

"Thus coming to me these wise souls
Are no more sent into earthly life
For they have attained to the highest.

Jun 21

"At day-break
All unmanifested become manifest,
And at night fall
The manifest return to unmanifest
And this occurs repeatedly.
But beyond all this
Is the unmanifested
Which is imperishable.

Jun 22

Beyond this cycle,
Out of this cycle,
There is an eternal being
That perishes not even when
All existence is destroyed,
Because it is, by nature,
Imperishable.

Jun 23

"Light and darkness are the two paths
Which are open to all forms of existence;
He who takes the path of light
Never returns to flesh-form.
The one who takes the path of darkness
Must return to flesh again and again.

Jun 24

"Those that join this imperishable Spirit,
Do not return anymore to earth,
Since they have reached my perfect home.

Jun 25

"Knowing this, the sage is not perplexed
But remains steadfast in devotion;
Disregarding the fruits of this life,
This sage works towards attaining
This everlasting peace."

Chapter Nine

Jun 26

Krishna continued:
"Now I will tell you
The profoundest secret,
Which, when followed,
Shall free you from doing wrong;
This is very pleasant
To the one who practices it.
Those that distrust it, however,
Will not find me
And so are destined
To come again and again
To earth in mortal frame.

Jun 27

"The whole world is pervaded by me
Yet my form is invisible;
All livings beings are rooted in me
Yet I am not rooted in them.

Jun 28

"Like the strong wind that moves everywhere
But rests only in space,
So all forms of life
Move around
But their only rest
Is with me.

Jun 29

"All beings at the end
Of every mortal cycle
Return into the realm of nature
Which is a part of me;
And at the start of the next cycle
I send them forth in mortal form
Again and again,
Whether the being
Desires birth or not;
His desire does not influence me.

Jun 30

"I am not attached to these acts
And they don't bind me,
Because I remain outside, unattached.

Jul 1

"The deluded ones despise me
When I am clad in human form,
Not realising that my real nature
Is as the Lord of all existence.

Jul 2

"These deluded ones possess
Ambitions that are vain,
Their acts are worthless,
And they possess futile knowledge,
And have faulty judgment.

Jul 3

"The wise ones worship me steadily
And remain undistracted
For they understand
That I am the imperishable.

Jul 4

"I am the ritual action,
I am the sacrifice,
I am the ancestral offering;
I am the medicinal herb,
I am the hymn.

Jul 5

"I am the melted butter,
I am also the fire
And the offering.

Jul 6

"I am the source of all life,
I am the universe,
The father, mother, grandfather,
The nurturer, and the purifier.
The pure.

Jul 7

"I am the OM,
I am the sacred scriptures,
I am the end, the goal,
I am the lord,
I am the home,
And the shelter.

Jul 8

"I am the friend,
And the origin,
I am life
And also death.

Jul 9

"I am a treasure-house
I am the imperishable seed
I am the heat in the sun
I can cause the rains to pour
And not cause the rains to pour.

Jul 10

"I am death
And yet deathlessness;
I am being
Yet non-being.

Jul 11

"Those that read the scriptures
And pray that I lead them
To eternal peace,
They reach where
The Supreme Spirit dwells
And they bask in the glory.

Jul 12

"Yet although those
Who read the scriptures
Enjoy this temporary glory,
When their merit is exhausted,
They are born again into mortal form
Because they merely followed
The letter of the scriptures
While they always sought
To fulfil their desires;
And so they depart
And return again and again.

Jul 13

"But if one worships me
Everywhere and always
I will safeguard whatever
Such a one attains.

Jul 14

"Even those that worship other gods
But who nevertheless
Worship with steady faith
They are worshipping me
Although not in the usual way.

Jul 15

"Whatever one offers to me,
Whether a leaf, a flower,
A fruit or water,
I accept it equally,
Only if it is offered with devotion
And with purity of mind.

Jul 16

"I am the same to all beings
I am unjust to none and hate none.

Jul 17

"Even if the greatest wrong-doer
Were to worship me with purity
I shall consider it righteous
Since such a one has rightly resolved.

Jul 18

"O Arjuna, my devotee
Is never lost nor loses,
Every person, whether man or woman,
Whether of high or low caste,
Can attain to me equally.

Jul 19

"Devote yourself to me,
Sacrifice to me,
Surrender to me,
Make me your goal,
And you will surely unite with me."

Chapter Ten

Jul 20

Krishna said:
"Neither the gods nor the sages
Know about my origin
Since I am their own source.

Jul 21

"The wise one who recognises me
As the unborn with neither beginning nor end,
Is released from all sins
Since he is stripped of all illusions.

Jul 22

"Intellect, knowledge, truth,
Freedom from illusions,
Forgiveness, self-control, calmness,
Pleasure and pain,
Birth and death,
All these spring from me.

Jul 23

"Fear and fearlessness,
Fame and failure,
These spring from me as well;
The one who understands this
Certainly attains perfect peace.

Jul 24

I am the source of all.
From me everything flows.
Therefore the wise worship me
With unwavering devotion.

Jul 25

"Harmlessness, equanimity,
Contentment, austerity,
Fame and failure
These, too, spring from me.
The one who comprehends this
Can attain complete peace.

Jul 26

"The wise who worship me with love
Are blessed by me as well;
All their darkness caused by ignorance
I destroy with the radiant beam of wisdom.

Jul 27

"I live in the hearts of the wise
And so I dispel their remaining ignorance
By throwing greater light on them."

Jul 28

Arjuna asked:
"You are the Supreme Spirit,
The eternal home, the unborn
And the omnipresent;
Can you show me the many manifestations
By which you pervade the world?
How shall I know you?
In my constant meditation,
My ears never tire of hearing
The words of nectar that
Emanate from your lips."

Jul 29

Krishna replied:
"O Arjuna, I preside in all hearts
Of all that is today or
All that once was.

Jul 30

"I am the beginning,
The middle
And the end.
Of the senses I am the mind,
Of beings I am the consciousness,
I am the seed of all existence.

Jul 31

"All the creative powers
Have been created by me.
I am the sun
Of all the luminaries;
I am the whirlwind of all winds.

Aug 1

"I am the hymn in the Vedas,
I am the potent force in nature,
I am the mind of the senses,
I am also the intelligence
In all that lives.

Aug 2

"I am the energy
In the fire, the earth,
The wind, the sky,
The heaven, the sun,
The moon and the planets.

Aug 3

"Of trees I am the fig-tree,
Among horses I am the horse born of nectar;
Of men I am the monarch.

Aug 4

"Of weapons I am the thunderbolt,
Of cows I am the cow of plenty;
Of those that procreate
I am the passionate force,
Of the serpents I am the cobra.

Aug 5

"I am the principle behind
All things that live in water,
I am the father of all fathers
And among rulers I am death.

Aug 6

"Of time I am the eternal present,
I am the lion among animals,
And the eagle among birds.

Aug 7

"Of warriors I am king Rama
Of fish I am the crocodile,
Among all the rivers in the world,
I am the Ganga.

Aug 8

"I am the beginning, the middle
And also the end of all creations;
I am the science of spirituality
Among all the sciences;
I am the discussion
Amongst those that debate.

Aug 9

"Of letters I am the alphabet 'a',
I am time inexhaustible;
I am the all-pervading preserver.

Aug 10

"I am devouring death,
I am the origin of all that will happen;
I am fame, fortune,
Speech, memory, intellect,
Constancy and forgiveness.

Aug 11

"I am the gambling of the cheat,
The splendour of the splendid,
I am victory,
I am effort,
I am the purity of the pure.

Aug 12

"I am the sceptre of rulers,
The strategy of conquerors,
The silence of mystery,
The wisdom of the sage.

Aug 13

"There is nothing moving or unmoving
That can exist without me.
But why do you need this knowledge?
I support the entire universe
Pervading it all
With but a fraction of my whole self."

Chapter Eleven

Aug 14

Arjuna said:
"Your words have blessed me
And dispelled the bewilderment
That had overcome me.
I believe all that you have said
And yet I long to have a vision
Of your divine form, in its infinity,
If only you think me worthy.
O Krishna, I beg of you
Do reveal yourself to me."

Aug 15

Krishna smiled :
"Behold my various forms
In countless hues and shapes
In countless wonders that
You have until now never seen.
In my body, behold the whole universe
In motion and yet motionless
And whatever else you wish to see.

Aug 16

"But since with mortal eyes
You cannot witness this bedazzling sight
I am endowing you with divine sight;
See now the glory of my power."

Aug 17

Sanjaya narrated to Dhritarashtra:
"Having thus spoken, then,
Krishna revealed to Arjuna his Supreme form.
Arjuna saw countless eyes and mouths,
Innumerable marvellous visions,
Countless shining ornaments
And raised flaming celestial weapons.

Aug 18

Wearing divine garlands
And various celestial garments
Covered by fragrant heavenly perfumes,
Embalmed with divine ointments,
Covered with wondrous things,
Resplendent, boundless, the Lord's face
Turned everywhere all at the same time.

Aug 19

If the light of a thousand suns
All at once, were to blaze
In the sky, simultaneously,
They might resemble mildly
What the wonder-struck Arjuna saw.

Aug 20

Arjuna saw the universe in manifold shapes
And all of them united to form the Divine Spirit.
Then with awe and fear,
With hair on end, head bowed low,
His hands clasped devoutly,
He addressed Krishna thus:

Aug 21

"I behold you in your infinite form
On all sides of me, around me,
With innumerable faces and eyes.
I see no end of you at all,
Nor any middle, nor any beginning,
I behold you with your sceptre, crown and discus,
All of them ablaze in full splendor.

Aug 22

"So radiant and blinding is your form,
I can hardly look upon you,
You are beyond human grasp.
The sight of you is too strong for me
Despite my special, divine sight.

Aug 23

You are imperishable,
The only one that must be sought,
The priceless treasure house of the world,
The guardian of the eternal life
And everlasting Spirit.

Aug 24

"Hosts of Gods enter you
And some in fear praise you
With folded hands;
And bands of great seers
Sing hymns to your glory
Crying out in praise of you.

Aug 25

"When I see you touching the sky
Glowing colorfully with open mouth
And wide-open fiery eyes,
I am terrified,
My courage and peace of mind
Have forsaken me, O Krishna.

Aug 26

"Seeing your stupendous form
With it's myriad faces,
Its innumerable eyes
And countless limbs, terrible jaws,
I am overwhelmed by what I see.

Aug 27

"I see all the sons of Dhritarashtra
Rushing headlong into your numerous mouths,
Which are all covered with sharp tusks.
For me all this is too awful to behold.

Aug 28

"Some of Dhritarashtra's sons
Are destroyed in your jaws,
With their heads crushed to tiny bits.

Aug 29

"As flooding rivers run
Furiously to join the ocean,
So too these heroes are flinging
Themselves into your flaming
And frightening mouths.

Aug 30

"As moths fly recklessly to the flame,
Only to destroy themselves in the attempt,
So do these men rush into your mouths
To be annihilated.

Aug 31

"You appear to swallow up the worlds
To surround them all over in flames.
Your glory permeates the universe
Your fiery rays mercilessly beat down
And hit the world irresistibly.

Sep 1

"Have mercy on me, O Krishna,
I wish to know you
Once again,
As I knew you before,
Since it is beyond me
To fathom your designs."

Sep 2

Krishna replied:
"I have shown you my destructive form
That is capable of laying waste
The whole world.
All these warriors gathered
On the Kauravas' side
Shall not escape justice.
So arise and gain good fame
Defeat your foes.

Sep 3

"I have already decided their fates.
You are but an instrument
It is not you that will be performing,
So go ahead and destroy them,
Fight them and fear not,
Your foes shall be crushed."

Sep 4

Arjuna prostrated himself before Krishna,
With hands folded religiously
And with a choking voice,
Bowing again and again
Addressed the Lord thus:

Sep 5

"It is right that the world
Rejoices in your name.
You are the wind,
You are death,
You are fire,
You are water,
You are moon,
You are father and grandfather,
Honor and glory to you,
A thousand and another thousand times.

Sep 6

"O lord Krishna, please forgive me
If I have said anything rash
Addressing you impudently,
As merely my friend
I was being familiar
And in my thoughtlessness
I overlooked your greatness.
Even if in jest I have insulted you
I beg you to pardon me!
I was ignorant and unknowing.
Please, O Krishna, I beseech you,
Take once again,
Your familiar form
I long to see you as you were before."

Sep 7

Krishna replied gently:
"My beloved friend, no other being
Has been allowed to see the vision
That I have allowed you to see;
Not even after a diligent study
Of the scriptures,
Not even by gifts or penance,
Nor by ritual or austerity,
Has it ever been possible
For man to see, O Arjuna,
What you have just seen.
Don't be afraid or confused by it,
Put away your fear and see me
Once again in the familiar form
Of your friend, the charioteer."

Sep 8

Sanjaya then narrated to Dhritarashtra
That the lord changed back
To becoming a charioteer once again.
Arjuna said:
"I am now relieved to see you thus
In the ordinary form such as my own
And I am once again calm."

Sep 9

Krishna replied:
"Only a person who is tirelessly
Devoted to me can see me and know me
He whose every action is done for me
To whom I am the final goal
Who loves me and hates none
O my dearest child,
Only he can realise me!"

Chapter Twelve

Sep 10

Arjuna, once again calm, asked:
"Tell me who is the better devotee
The one that worships you
Or the one that knows you
As a personal god
Or the one that tries to know you
As the imperishable?"

Sep 11

Krishna said:
"Those devotees that keep
Their mind fixed on me,
Who honour me
With their unwavering faith,
Those are the very best.

Sep 12

"Those that honour me
As indestructible,
The indefinable,
The omnipresent,
The imponderable,
Those that suppress their base senses
And view life's ups and downs with equipoise,
Working for the welfare of others
Surely they find their way to me.

Sep 13

"Those that surrender their actions to me
Thinking on me, worshipping me,
With no other thought
But every thought
Focused only on me,
I rescue them quickly
From the perpetual
Cycles of birth and death.

Sep 14

"So Arjuna, keep your mind
Ever fixed on me,
But if you are unable to do so,
Keep practicing it nevertheless,
But if you cannot concentrate,
Devote yourself to my service
Do everything for my sake
And you will reach the desired goal.

Sep 15

"But if you are too weak
Even for this,
Then do everything dutifully
But don't ever think
Of receiving any fruit
From your action.

Sep 16

"Knowledge is better
Than blind action,
Meditation is better
Than knowledge,
Renunciation is better
Than meditation
And on renouncing immediately,
At once, you will achieve,
Infinite and boundless peace.

Sep 17

"The one who is incapable of hatred
And who is compassionate and unselfish,
Without any kind of arrogance,
Reacting calmly
To both pain and pleasure,
And is moreover, forgiving by nature,
Always content, always controlled and determined,
With mind devoted to me
Such a devotee is beloved to me.

Sep 18

"The one who harms none
Whom, in turn,
The world cannot harm,
Such a one is my favorite, O Arjuna.

Sep 19

"The one who expects nothing,
Is beyond both joy and hatred
Who neither grieves nor desires
That one is my beloved.

Sep 20

"Indifferent to praise and criticism
Being content with silence,
The one who calmly regards
All that occurs and transpires,
That one is dear to me."

Chapter Thirteen

Sep 21

Arjuna asked:
"Please, O Krishna, explain to me
About God and Nature
Matter and Self
Wisdom and what must be understood."

Sep 22

Krishna replied:
"The body is the playground
Of the infinite, real Self;
And that which understands the nature
Of matter is called the Self.
I am the omniscient Self
That resides in this playground
And knowledge of both,
Matter and Self,
Is called wisdom.

Sep 23

"This playground, which is matter,
Consists of five elements,
Earth, fire, air, water and ether;
Then, it also contains the ten senses
Hearing, sight, smell, touch and taste,
Hands, feet, tongue and the two organs
Of excretion and reproduction,
Then the mind,
Then the five sensations,
Desire, hatred, pleasure,
Pain and sympathy;
The desire for survival and vitality
All these are the constituents of matter.

Sep 24

"Humility, sincerity,
Forgiveness, rectitude
Purity, devotion
Steadfastness and self-control
Renunciation of sensuousness,
Absence of pride,
Understanding of birth and death
Comprehension of old age and sickness,
A constant thirst to know the self,
And always seeking the truth,
That one alone who possesses
These qualities can be called wise,
All else is ignorance.

Sep 25

"The great spirit, the truth, exists everywhere
Sees everything, hears all,
Dwells everywhere, is within all beings,
And yet is removed from them,
Motionless while being in motion,
Too subtle to be seen,
Too far and yet always near.
This truth is the light of all lights
Beyond any reach of darkness,
And it exists in all hearts.

Sep 26

"Nature and God have no beginning
Nature is the law which has generated
Cause and effect
The spirit dwells within man's body
Which is nothing but matter,
And those that understand both,
Body and the self,
They alone can be free
From rebirth

Sep 27

"Some realise the truth by meditation
Others by reasoning, still others by righteous action
Still others merely believe without personal knowledge
But if they perform rightly,
True to the truth,
They too cross over to the other side
Going beyond the cycle of rebirth.

Sep 28

"The one that can see the supreme in all,
Seeing the imperishable in the perishable,
Knowing that it is nature alone acting,
And never the spirit,
Such a one alone truly understands.

Sep 29

"Perceiving that all forms of life
Are rooted finally in one,
However diverse they might be,
Such a one can indeed
Meet the Absolute.

Sep 30

"The Supreme Spirit
Though present in all forms
Retains its purity unalloyed
Unaffected by anything.

Oct 1

"As the sun throws light on the whole world
So the Supreme Spirit pervades the whole universe.

Chapter Fourteen

Oct 2

Lord Krishna continued:
"Through whichever womb people are born
It is the Supreme Spirit that conceives
And I am the creator of all creation.

Oct 3

"Purity, passion and ignorance,
Are the three qualities brought forth by nature
They influence the free spirit of all.

Oct 4

"Purity being bright and strong,
Ties one down by its hankering
After enlightenment,
By its attachment to tranquillity, peace.

Oct 5

"Passion created by a desire
For pleasure and attachment
Binds the soul
Through its obsession with activity.

Oct 6

"But ignorance born of darkness,
Dulls the senses,
Binding with chains of folly,
And laziness and apathy.

Oct 7

"Those that are pure rise upwards.
The passionate remain in the middle,
While, the dull, steeped in apathy,
Sink downwards.

Oct 8

"Purity brings happiness,
Passion brings chaos
Ignorance leads to failure;
Purity can prevail
When the other two fail.

Oct 9

"With purity the light of knowledge
Burns forth from every pore
Of the body.
And when purity prevails
The soul passes to the purest regions
Beyond birth and death.

Oct 10

"When passion dominates,
The soul is reborn amongst
Those who are active
In their greed and avarice.

Oct 11

"When ignorance prevails
The soul enters
The womb of the ignorant.

Oct 12

"Purity creates wisdom,
Passion creates greed,
Ignorance creates foolish darkness.

Oct 13

"The one who regards alike both clay and gold,
And who neither likes nor dislikes,
Such a one can become
One with the Supreme.

Oct 14

"Know that I alone house
The Supreme Spirit,
And eternal righteousness,
And infinite joy.

Chapter Fifteen

Oct 15

"The wise attain freedom from re-birth
When, freed from pride and delusion,
They have conquered
Their love for sense-objects;
Renouncing them
They concentrate on the self
And then they cease to be deluded
And troubled
By pleasure and pain.

Oct 16

"There, with the real Self,
Neither the sun,
Nor the moon
Nor fire blaze.
Those that find
Themselves there
Never return to this world.

Oct 17

"When the Supreme Spirit leaves the body
It takes the senses and the mind along
As easily as the wind which
While passing through flowers
Gathers perfume.

Oct 18

"The ignorant do not perceive
That it is indeed the Supreme Spirit
That is present in life
And departs at death;
Only the wise can perceive its nature.
The saints, after great efforts,
Find this spirit in themselves
But not so
The unwise.

Oct 19

"Both the sun and moon get their light
From me alone,
I am the origin,
I animate the world with my vitality;
And the plants, too,
Receive their nourishment from me.

Oct 20

"There are two aspects of nature,
The perishable and the imperishable.
All life in this world belongs to the former
The latter alone is myself.

Oct 21

"I am higher than all,
I pervade the world
And uphold everything.
And so I have revealed to you
My most mystic knowledge.

Chapter Sixteen

Oct 22

"The one that can be called righteous
Possesses these qualities:
Fearlessness, purity of mind,
Wisdom, a giving nature,
Self-control, a sacrificing attitude,
He studies the scriptures,
Exercises austerity,
Is incapable of mindless harm,
And is also incapable of anger.

Oct 23

"This wise one is capable of renunciation,
Is contented, he is averse to being critical,
He is compassionate to living beings,
And is free from greed,
But he is courteous, modest and sincere

Oct 24

"Being brave, and forgiving,
Free from both hate and vanity,
Such a one possesses godly qualities.

Oct 25

"The one who has godless qualities
Possesses hypocrisy, pride and insolence
Is cruel and ignorant.

Oct 26

"Godly qualities lead to freedom
And godless ones lead to bondage.
Don't be anxious, O Arjuna,
You possess godly qualities.

Oct 27

"The godless ones know neither
How to act nor how to renounce.
They have neither purity nor truth,
They do not know right conduct.

Oct 28

"They say that the universe is an accident,
With no purpose and no God,
That life is created out of desire alone.
Thus these souls rise to become
Enemies of the world,
Capable of destruction.

Oct 29

"Full of hypocrisy and insatiable desire,
Possessing excessive pride and arrogance,
Holding wrong views,
They act unrighteously.

Oct 30

"They seek gratification of desire
As their highest goal,
Caught in a hundred vain hopes
They accumulate wealth
Unjustly procured
In order to pander to their sensual desires.

Oct 31

"They think thus:
I have gained this today,
That tomorrow shall be mine;
I have destroyed one enemy,
I will destroy others as well,
I am perfect, powerful and rich,
Who is there to match me ?

Nov 1

"Thus blinded by ignorance
Trapped by desire,
This one moves further down
In the cycle of rebirth

Nov 2

"Vain, stubborn, proud and arrogant,
These ones perform meaningless rituals
Disregarding all decency.
Such people that disown and dislike me
Their fate is continuous rebirth.

Nov 3

"Lust, anger and greed
Must all be forsaken,
Since it is they that keep you chained
To this cycle of repeated rebirth.

Nov 4

"He who has given up these
Reaches the highest state;
But the one who disregards the scriptures
Will not attain either perfection,
Or happiness
Or the final goal.

Nov 5

"Thus, O Arjuna,
Whenever you doubt about the path to choose.
Always be guided by the holy books
Because there you will obtain
True guidance.

Chapter Seventeen

Nov 6

Arjuna asked:
"Those that perform sacrifices,
Not according to the scriptures
But yet with implicit faith,
Are they pure,
Or passionate
Or ignorant ?"

Nov 7

Lord Krishna answered:
"It has to be one of the three.
Now I will explain.
By nature every being has faith
The pure worship
The Supreme Spirit;
The passionate worship
Wealth and magic for their powers;
The ignorant revere
Spirits and ghosts.

Nov 8

"Those who are slaves
To hypocrisy and egoism
Are motivated by desire and passion
And thus are devoted to evil.

Nov 9

"The food that men ingest
Is of three kinds:
The pure ones choose food
That enriches and prolongs life,
Gives vigor, happiness and cheer.
Those in whom passion dominates,
Like bitter, sour, salty, pungent foods.
These produce pain, grief and disease.
The food that is poor in nutrition,
And which is stale and unclean,
Is the food preferred by the apathetic.

Nov 10

"Sacrifice, similarly, is like this:
When it is offered by one who doesn't ask
For any fruit,
Performing only according to the scriptures
and with implicit faith
That one is pure.

Nov 11

"Sacrifice that is done
For results or for vanity
Is the product of passion.

Nov 12

"That sacrifice which is performed
Against the scriptures,
Done without prayers and faith
Is indulged in by the ignorant.

Nov 13

"There are three kinds of penance;
Where the gods, teachers and the wise
Are revered with purity
That one is the penance of the body.
The one where speech hurts none,
And which is true and pleasant to hear
And beneficial to the listener
That is the penance of speech.
Serenity, gentleness, silence,
Self-control, a pure mind,
These are the penance of the mind.
These three penances,
Performed with faith,
And without desire for return,
These may be considered pure.

Nov 14

"But penance done with hypocrisy,
Or done for popularity or vanity,
Arising out of a desire for reward
Can be called penance
Arising out of passion.

Nov 15

"And penance performed
At the wrong place
And at the wrong time
And to the wrong person,
With the wrong attitude
Arises out of ignorance.

Nov 16

"Om tat sat is the triple designate
Of the Supreme Spirit
By which all ceremonials
And sacrifices are ordained.

Nov 17

"All acts of sacrifice, penance,
According to the scriptures,
Must always begin with the word 'Om'.
Those that seek salvation must utter
'Tat' without aiming for any reward.
'Sat' means the ultimate reality,
And it is used for praiseworthy action.
Also an action done for the lord
Is called 'sat'
As well as those actions that are performed
With steadfast faith
And with deep conviction.

Nov 18

"Whatever is undertaken
Without faith or sincerity,
Whether it be a sacrifice or anything else
Is 'asat', untruth.
For it is a negation of 'sat', truth.
Such an act, with 'asat' has no value
Either here or hereafter."

Chapter Eighteen

Nov 19

Arjuna asked:
"Can you tell me the difference
Between relinquishing
And renunciating ?"

Nov 20

"The lord answered:
Some wise men say that renunciation implies
Foregoing an action which arises from desire,
And that relinquishing requires
The surrendering of the fruit.
Some philosophers say that since
All action is evil it should be abandoned;
Others say that acts of sacrifice
Benevolence and austerity
Must not be given up.
O Arjuna, listen to my explanation
Of this matter which is three-fold.

Nov 21

"Acts of sacrifice, austerity and benevolence
Must not be given up, but must be performed
Since they help purify the soul;
But they must be undertaken
With detachment
And with no thought for reward.

Nov 22

"The one who performs an obligatory action
Believing it to be a duty,
Having no interest in doing it or in its reward,
Such an act of renunciation
Can be defined as pure.

Nov 23

"The wise one does not refrain
From doing his duty because it would be painful
Nor does this one do it because it would bring joy;
But he does so merely because it must be done.
The fruit of action for him
Is never the motivation.

Nov 24

"For any action to take place
There must be five causes:
The body,
The personality,
The physical organs,
Their functions
And destiny.

Nov 25

"He who is unspoilt by attachment
"Even if a man devoid of attachment
Kills another living being,
He does not really kill him,
Nor do his acts bind him down
To the cycle of rebirth.

Nov 26

"He who knows that one indestructible spirit
Pervades in all beings,
May be called a pure knowledgeable one.

Nov 27

"The one who thinks that all existence
Is separate and unconnected,
Is nothing but a passionate performer.

Nov 28

"But the one who clings blindly to one idea,
As if it were everything,
Without logic or truth
Is the one who is ignorant.

Nov 29

"Any act done disinterestedly,
Without concern for reward,
Is a pure act.

Nov 30

"But even if an act is done most enthusiastically
But the doer is motivated by reward or vanity.
Such an act may be considered passionate.

Dec 1

"An act undertaken by delusion
And seeing wrong as right
Can be called an ignorant act.

Dec 2

"When someone has no vanity,
And no desire for reward,
But possesses only courage and confidence,
Caring little about the outcome
Whether he will be successful or a failure,
That person acts out of purity.

Dec 3

"The one who is desirous of reward,
And causes unnecessary harm,
Has impure thoughts,
And is always tossing between joy and sorrow,
Such an individual
Has a 'passionate' nature.

Dec 4

"On the other hand,
He who is unsteady,
Base, stubborn, deceitful, malicious,
Lazy and despondent
And always putting things off,
Such a one is surrounded by darkness
And can be called 'dull'.

Dec 5

"There are three kinds of understanding:
I will explain them to you fully:
The intellect that understands
The creation and destruction of life,
Understanding which actions
Need to be performed and which not,
The intellect that understands
What must be feared and what must not,
And discerns the difference
Between bondage and freedom,
That intellect is of a pure understanding.

Dec 6

"That intellect which cannot
Discern between right and wrong,
What ought to be done
And what ought not to be done,
That intellect can be regarded
As of a passionate nature.

Dec 7

"That intellect which is covered in darkness,
Sees wrong as right,
Sees all things in a perverse light,
That intellect is dictated by dullness.

Dec 8

"The steady mind which has both
Vitality and senses in check,
That mind is of a pure nature.

Dec 9

"The mind that is motivated by material reward
Concerned with pleasure and wealth,
Performing rituals for rewards
That mind is of a passionate nature.

Dec 10

"The mind that clings perversely to false notions,
Fear, grief, despair and vanity,
That mind is of a dull and dark nature.

Dec 11

"O Arjuna, happiness is of three kinds.
One where an individual finds
That it increases day-by-day
And delivers one from misery,
Which at first seems like poison
But afterwards acts like nectar,
That happiness is pure,
Being born out of wisdom.

Dec 12

"That happiness that first seems like nectar
But later acts like a poison
That pleasure is one that arises out of passion,
And is born out of desire.

Dec 13

"That happiness which, at first,
Lulls the senses, springs out of laziness,
Lethargy and folly,
That happiness comes
Out of ignorance.

Dec 14

"There is no being on the earth
Or in the other worlds that is free
From one of these three qualities,
Purity, passion and dullness,
Since they are all created by nature.

Dec 15

"O Arjuna, everybody's acts
Are fixed according to the dominant quality
Of their nature.
Man's outward life
Must express his inward being.

Dec 16

"Perfection is attained when all
Perform what is their specific duty.

Dec 17

"If all beings were to remember
The being that pervades the world
And worship it,
By a correct performance of duties
They would all attain perfection.

Dec 18

"It is better, by far,
To do one's own duty,
However imperfectly one may do it,
Than to do the duty of another,
However well it may be performed.
One does not incur sin when one does
What one is supposed to do,
Ordained by one's own innate nature.
One must never forsake the duty
That is meant for one's own nature
Even if it is defective
Since all acts are clouded
As fire is clouded by smoke.

Dec 19

"He who is unattached everywhere
Who has subdued the baser self
And from whom desire has fled
That one can reach the Supreme Spirit
Where no further action remains to be done.

Dec 20

"Let me tell you how to attain perfection.
One must be guided by pure reason,
And be firmly restrained,
One must turn away from sense-objects
And give up attachment and hatred;
One must constantly possess
The spirit of renunciation.
One must abandon selfishness,
The lust for power,
And the spirit of arrogance.
By abandoning anger and desire,
By possessing nothing of one's own,
Having attained peace,
Such a one is ready
To join the eternal Spirit.

Dec 21

"And when such a person
Unites with the Spirit
There is no feeling of desire or regret
And he can then reside in the eternal home.
Thus, surrendering thoughts and actions
Both to me,
Regarding me as the Supreme ,
And being steadfast in your faith,
You will cross over all difficulties easily.

But if, from vanity,
You disregard what I say,
You will get even deeper
In the cycle of rebirth.

Dec 22

"If, therefore, indulging in such thoughts,
You say, 'I will not fight',
O beloved Arjuna,
You will see the futility of such a resolve,
Because your innate nature will triumph
And compel you,
Almost against your will,
To do your righteous duty.

The Supreme resides in all hearts
Making them move by its power.
So, surrendering yourself to the great power,
Do your duty and hasten towards
The eternal home.

Dec 23

"My last words to you on this subject are these:
You are my beloved, my friend
And I am your well-wisher;
Dedicate yourself to me, worship me,
Sacrifice all for me,
Fix your mind on me.

Dec 24

"Prostrate yourself before me,
And you will definitely come
To the eternal home.
I promise you this,
Because you are indeed dear to me.

Dec 25

"Do not be anxious,
You are only doing what is your duty
And therefore there
Shall be no sin committed.

Dec 26

"Do not discuss this with those persons
Who have not sacrificed
Or those that are not austere in their lives
Or those who have no devotion in them
Or those that mock or speak ill of me.

Dec 27

"But the one who teaches
This to the devotees
Such a one shall merge with me.
The one who studies
Our spiritual discourses
Who thereby worships me
Shall doubtless, come to me.

Dec 28

"The one who listens
To these discourses with faith,
Without doubt,
That one, too,
Shall be freed from evil
And attain to the happy world
Of all the righteous.

Dec 29

"Tell me, O Arjuna, have my answers
Dispelled your fears and doubts,
Shattering all your delusions ?"

Dec 30

Arjuna replied:

"Yes, my doubts have cleared
And my delusions have vanished
The light has dawned
And I stand before you
Ready to do your will."

Dec 31

Sanjaya concluded:
"Thus have I heard the discussion
Between Arjuna and Krishna
That has raised my hair on end.
The more I ponder on these glorious words,
The more I find myself lost in joy.
I am reminded again and again
Of the lord's unmatched beauty
And I am filled with amazement
And endless happiness.
Wherever there is Krishna,
The lord of wisdom,
And wherever there is Arjuna,
The great warrior,
There surely will be good fortune,
Welfare and righteousness."

Bibliography

1. The Bhagavadgita by S. Radhakrishnan
2. The Bhagavad Gita by Sri Sankaracharya
3. Bhagavad-Gita As It Is by Swami Prabhupada
4. The Gita According to Gandhi by Mahadev Desai
5. The Bhagavadgita by P. Lal
6. Srimad Bhagavad-Gita by Swami Vireswarananda
7. Secret of Action- Swami Chinmayananda
8. Krishna, the Man and his Philosophy by Osho
9. The Bhagavad Gita by Annie Besant
10. The Geeta by Shri Purohit Swami
11. Bhagavad Gita by C.Rajagopalachari
12. The Bhagavad Gita by Dilip Kumar Roy
13. The Bhagavad Gita by Ramesh Balsekar
14. Art of Man Making - Geeta talks by Swami Chinmayananda
15. Talks with Sri Ramana Maharshi by Sri Ramanasramam
16. The Song Celestial: Bhagavad Gita by Sir Edwin Arnold
17. Who's Who in the Mahabharata by Subhash Mazumdar

BOOKS OF RELATED INTEREST FROM NAB

REALIZATION OF THE SUPREME SELF

The Bhagavad Gita Yogas

Trevor Leggett

ISBN: 81-7822-071-7

BHAGAVAD-GITA

Combined with his Essays on the Gita

William Quan Judge

ISBN: 81-7822-096-2

GITA FOR SUCCESS IN MODERN LIFE

From Basement to Board Room

R.S. Garg

ISBN: 81-7822-125-x

THE GITA FOR THE 21ST CENTURY

Satya Prakash Agarwal

ISBN: 81-7822-153-5

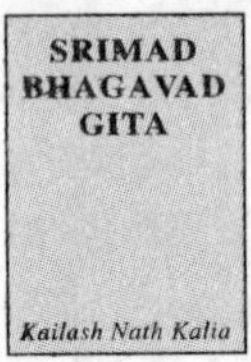

SRIMAD BHAGAVAD GITA

Kailash Nath Kalia

ISBN: 81-7822-274-4

THE BHAGAVAD GITA

Alan Jacobs

ISBN: 81-7822-241-8